Radical Purity

Simple Steps to Protect a Pure Lifestyle

David Edwards

Revivalism

Copyright

Endorsement

This quick read is just long enough to make it easy for repeated reading, and practical enough to actually help its readers live lives of radical purity free from sin. This book is not for everybody though. If you're content to stay in a rut, you probably won't benefit from Dave's book. If you want to bring lasting change into your life, you'll be provided great mind renewal with this book.

Steve Bremner

Missionary to
Peru

Host
Fire On Your Head Podcast

Author
Nine Lies People Believe About Speaking in Tongues

Contents

Before You Read — 7

Recognition — 11

Foreword — 13

1. The Pure Source — 15

2. What is Purity? — 25

3. Practical Steps to Purity — 41

4. The Purpose of Purity — 55

5. The Power of Purity — 71

6. Dangers of Impurity — 81

7. Protecting Purity — 97

About the Author —113

Resources —115

Before You Read

Sensitive Material

This book contains mature content and sensitive subject matter; therefore, it is not recommended for younger readers.

Study Question Answers

The answers to the study questions are either in bold or underlined section headings within the corresponding chapters.

Allessia

Your purity is my strength

...

<u>Recognition</u>

My own walk in purity has many friendships that provide me with strength and encouragement. These brothers elevate me up when I find I am at my lowest. I am eternally grateful for all of their support over the years: Damian McCrink, Brandon Weaver, Bryan Jackson, Keith Collins, and Tom Roan. Special thanks go to Scott Thompson and Jeremy Connor for being there for me—day in and day out. We bear our armor together as we raise our swords to the sky.

Sheryl Roan, you have been generous in your support and encouragement. Thank you for taking the time to edit this book.

Special thanks to Scott Thompson for writing the Foreword and Steve Bremner for endorsing the book.

Foreword

David Edwards is a close friend of mine and someone I run with to advance the Kingdom. His passion for revival and love for Jesus are contagious. This book will both challenge and equip you to live in purity that is not out of works, but the fruit of a relationship with our loving Savior.

Purity is an important topic for believers today. With more opportunity to stumble than ever before through technology and culture, this book couldn't have come at a better time. I would love to see this book as a read for youth, college, and adult groups. It would be a great book to go through with others who can lock arms with you in accountability, and forward movement in your "living from the Pure

Source." This book can be a catalyst to see a change from a losing fight to a victorious march forward in purity. I wholeheartedly recommend and endorse this book.

Scott Thompson

Senior Team
Jesus Culture

Author
***Words of Knowledge
Made Easy***

1

The Pure Source

My desire in writing this book is to help establish and protect a lifestyle of purity. I try to take a different approach on the matter; one which asks "why" we must live in purity and gives practical steps for "how" to attain a pure lifestyle. Hopefully, the answers will give us new insight and ability to live purely. For too long, purity has been something that we seemingly force upon ourselves. True purity is a transformation inside that echoes to the outside. We become pure through drinking from the life of Jesus—the Source of all purity. This internal change is reflected in our exterior actions, capturing the attention of others, and awakening their need to drink from the Well of Eternal Life.

Let us take a look at the amazing story of the "woman at the well." She ventures to get water for her physical body, but ends up quenching the thirst of her spirit when she encounters Jesus. This encounter made her a source of water for her city.

> A woman from Samaria came to draw water. Jesus said to her, "Give me a drink."... The Samaritan woman said to him, "How is it that you, a Jew, ask for a drink from me, a woman of Samaria?" (For Jews have no dealings with Samaritans.)

Jesus answered her, "If you knew the gift of God, and whom it is that is saying to you, 'Give me a drink,' you would have asked him, **and he would have given you living water.**"

The woman said to him, "Sir, you have nothing to draw water with, and the well is deep. Where do you get that living water? Are you greater than our father Jacob? He gave us the well and drank from it himself, as did his sons and his livestock."

Jesus said to her, "Everyone who drinks of this water will be thirsty again, but whoever drinks of the water that I will give him will never be thirsty again. **The water that I will give him will become in him a spring of water welling up to eternal life.**" The woman said to him, "Sir, give me this water, so that I will not be thirsty or have to come here to draw water."

John 4:7-15 ESV, *emphasis mine*

Soaked with purity, His words cause her to begin to thirst for the substance of His life. She has never tasted such refreshing water—soothing to her soul. She requests another drink in order to satisfy this new feeling bubbling-up inside her. Without realizing it, she had been splashed with the Origin of Life.

"Jesus said to her, "Go, call your husband, and come here." The woman answered him, "I have no husband." Jesus said to her, "You are right in saying, 'I have no husband'; for you have had five husbands, and the one you now have is not your husband. What you have said is true." The woman said to him, "Sir, I perceive that you are a prophet."

vv 16-19

The life she ingests by asking Jesus questions results in a response that washes away her impurities. Jesus then reveals to her that He is the Messiah. This revelation turns her encounter into a relationship—keeping her connected to the Pure Source. This connection makes her a well, supplying the life of Jesus to her village.

"So the woman left her water jar and went away into town and said to the people, "Come, see a man who told me all that I ever did. Can this be the Christ?" They went out of the town and were coming to him."

vv 28-30

She found the True Source. **Jesus is the Purest Source of water in the universe.** Likewise, when we drink from the Pure Source, we too will begin a relationship with Jesus that will wash us clean from the inside out. Her road to freedom began with Jesus drawing water from her. This illustrates how we relate to Him. She wasn't required to quit her immoral behavior before He would introduce Himself to her. Rather, He introduces Himself to her, causing her to draw from Him instead of the impure sources. Once this happens, she is easily made free from her impure behavior.

The goal of this book is to cause us to live from the One Pure Source—Jesus. He satisfies every need, every desire, and every thirst deep within our souls. Just as the woman became a well of eternal water, we too are living wells of pure water.

Conclusion

I will not attempt to cover all the areas which one may encounter when dealing with the subject of purity. This manuscript is designed to be a quick and handy resource-guide to help us navigate safely back to pure waters when the storms of temptations arise, and to make us aware of the schemes of the devil, which are aimed at luring us into impurity. When we are aware of his plans, we can then take an offensive and radical approach, one that will prevent temptations even before they arise. We will begin in the next chapter by defining purity.

<u>Study Questions</u>

What kind of Water did the Samaritan Woman ask Jesus for?

What does the water that Jesus gives to someone become?

Who is the Pure Source?

<u>Notes</u>

2

What is Purity?

Lately, at Bethel Atlanta School of Supernatural Ministry, where I serve as a pastor and teacher, we have been focusing on the theme of purity. What is purity? What does it mean to live pure? It can be categorized in many ways, but generally, purity is examined in relation to sexuality.

Defining Purity

I searched through Google for the definitions of purity, of which, there are many. **The most common themes were; the "quality of being pure," and the idea of not being "tainted," like finding a pure source of water that is free of pollutants.** The definitions then began to describe purity as it relates to modern thought: being pure as in being good—as opposed to evil, and physical purity like maintaining chastity and virginity.

I believe these definitions introduce the subject well. It is important to understand its meaning, especially how most of us perceive it. However, with this definition, many of us—specifically as Christians, find ourselves in a war to maintain a "standard." Therefore, anytime we "fall short" of this standard we end up feeling like the "scum of the earth" and unworthy followers of Christ. The purity He exemplifies is complete, but it often feels unattainable. Ironically, we find ourselves trying to match our level of purity with His, rather than embracing His purity as our own.

Fighting the War

Is this accurate? Have you ever felt this way? Do you feel this way right now as you read these paragraphs? I know I feel this way often. Unfortunately, we sometimes make decisions that are impure. These decisions can lead to impure thoughts; impure thoughts can lead to impure actions; impure actions can lead to sins. Once we realize we've sinned, hope usually isn't the first thing that goes through our minds, "Right?" Isn't it usually condemnation? "Yeah, I've eaten that sandwich about a thousand times!"

The heart of the Father is a heart of restoration. In fact, He has restored all things in Jesus. Therefore, if we sin, the Father's heart towards us isn't to "let us have-it"; rather, His heart every-time is to restore us and lift us higher. I used to get depressed for days after a bout with impurity. If I looked at something lustful, pornographic, or impure, then I was undone. I was in the doldrums. I felt like a wretched "Christian," as I thought to myself, "How can I follow Christ and do these things?" I became miserable. I failed to see purity as His gift to me. All-the-time, however, God wasn't blasting me with condemnation; He was trying to get me to realize that He had already paid for the sins I committed. This payment has forever made me "righteous." The battle was in the mind. I needed to realize who I was in Christ. This realization brings restoration.

What about Repentance?

Repentance means to change the way we think. The transforming of the mind here is repentance. When I stop thinking about how bad I've been, and start thinking about all that Jesus has done in me, then I can view myself from a heavenly perspective. This creates a heart-change and opens our eyes to His forgiveness. Seeing things from the paradigm of heaven is living from a pure source. Living from this pure source transforms the mind and makes us pure.

Pray then like this:

Our Father in heaven,
hallowed be your name.
Your kingdom come,
Your will be done,

on earth as it is in heaven.

Matthew 6:9-10 ESV

"Holy" means "set apart," or, more accurately, "otherworldly." **Holiness is otherworldliness.** It is living from His world. Like the Samaritan women, we must remain connected to the living water. This is the proper flow. Our spiritual lives govern our mental and physical lives. With this in proper alignment, we will have the necessary vantage point to overcome impure temptations whenever they emerge.

The Stronghold of the Mind

One time, I was searching on the computer for something that normally wouldn't yield provocative results. (Obviously, media is a place we must guard our hearts.) Suddenly a picture of a beautiful woman wearing see-through attire appeared. The image shot straight into my soul like an "arrow" or "fiery dart" (Eph 6:16). I quickly scrolled down so the image was no longer on the screen. I had victory over the first thought. Next, out of nowhere, a second thought occurred. "Why don't you just scroll back through and take another glance?" As I thought about it, I found myself doing it. Ouch! I responded to the thought without even "thinking" about it. The mind is a pivotal platform from which we can either fly high or free fall. Thankfully, God got me out of "that one" before more temptations could sabotage my way of thinking.

The House of Thoughts

In that instant, Holy Spirit showed me that the initial thought was like the first piece of wood used in the building of a house. To give it a second thought is like adding another timber to the construction. Soon, the thoughts are framed into walls. Walls form rooms, and hold up the structure of the house. A house of thoughts creates a place for action to be given to those thoughts. This action is usually a doorway for sin to enter our lives. This pattern can turn the house into a stronghold in the mind. If this pattern is left unresolved, it may get worse, and invite demonic influence.

> For though we walk in the flesh, we are not waging war according to the flesh. For the weapons of our warfare are not of the flesh but have divine power to destroy strongholds. We destroy arguments and every lofty opinion raised against the knowledge of God, and take every thought captive to obey Christ.

> 2 Corinthians 10:4-5 ESV

Wow, Paul illustrates this with perfection! The war of temptation cannot be fought with the flesh. Approaching it this way causes us to stumble, or gives us a false sense of victory. The power we possess is supernatural. It can tear down strongholds in the mind, as well as prevent their foundation from ever being laid.

An impure thought is an "opinion" or "argument" against the knowledge of God. The "Knowledge of God" is heaven-first thinking. Thinking like this causes our earthly actions to mirror heavenly actions. The outcome is the supernatural ability to take "every thought captive." This keeps the house of temptation from being built in our minds. It also halts a pattern from developing that leads to strongholds. When our interior is made strong, then our exterior actions will be made strong as well. The answer isn't in destroying the computer; it's in destroying the lies in the mind that would tempt you to look at something impure on the computer.

Live from the Spirit

Listen as you read the following quote from John G. Lake as he describes how we were meant to live from the spirit:

> In the beginning, man's spirit was the dominant force in the world; when he sinned his *mind* became dominant. Sin dethroned the spirit and crowned the intellect. But grace is restoring the spirit to its place of dominion, and when man comes to realize this, he will live in the realm of the supernatural without effort. No longer will faith be a struggle, but a normal living in the realm of God ...

Man's intellect is ever conscious of supernatural forces that he cannot understand. He senses the spirit realm and longs for its freedom and creative power, but cannot enter until changed from self and sin; the spirit enthroned and in action rather than the intellect—spirit above *both mind and matter*.

[This excerpt is from *John G. Lake: The Complete Collection of His Life Teachings*, by Roberts Liardon.]

This is life in the spirit. God is Spirit, and we, like Him, are first spirit. When our spirits are led by the Holy Spirit then the pull of the mind and flesh, in association with the temptation to act or think impure, is annihilated.

Conclusion

What is purity? It is living, thinking, and acting from the Source, from Jesus, and from heavenly places. On that note, I'll end this chapter with two verses of triumph:

> And [He] raised us up with him and seated us with him in the heavenly places in Christ Jesus.
>
> Ephesians 2:6 ESV

> But we have the mind of Christ.
>
> 1 Corinthians 2:16b

In this chapter, we have been dealing with the rough places in life, and considering purity in ways we may have overlooked in our attempts to attain freedom in the past. The only way to truly overcome such areas is to admit you need help. Don't fight the battle on your own. If we have thoughts that seek to dethrone our heavenly place, we must realize that we have the higher ground. Resist and the enemies of our souls will flee. Simply flush the tempting thoughts and keep going. Remember, you have the mind of Christ and are at the right hand of the Son of God.

<u>Study Questions</u>

What is Purity?

What is Holiness?

What is an impure thought?

<u>Notes</u>

3

Practical Steps to Purity

How do we stay pure? I think this is a question that many of us entertain almost on a daily basis. In the last chapter, I wrote about how living in purity is living from a heavenly source that transforms our minds to make pure decisions. Living from this Source reverses our desire to live from the lusts of the flesh. Repentance is then activated as our thought processes are changed to think like Jesus. This is great in theory and is the foundation of pure living, but I wanted to follow it up with some "real life" ways we can walk it out on a daily basis. Here are some practical steps that will provide an exit-ramp for us when temptations seem too difficult to overcome.

1. <u>Transform Your Mind</u>

We must have our minds in the right place—a heavenly place—if they are going to tell our bodies how to respond properly to the given situation that we may either on purpose or inadvertently find ourselves in. This is the foundation for success. A Christ-like mentality will cause us to view something impure as a contaminant, rather than viewing it as a pleasure. This point-of-view will give rise to a heavenly response, removing an earthly or fleshly reaction. Therefore, more often than not, we will find ourselves in victory rather than in recovery.

2. <u>Don't Take a Second Look</u>

Most areas of impurity are gravitated towards our sexuality, whether male or female. We are created with God given sex drives. It is an incorrect answer to pretend like these drives do not exist; instead, we must guide them in ways that produce pure fulfillments. The eyes are one of the ways we experience pleasure. Because of this, if we see something attractive and neglect to manage it from a source of purity, the image may lead to impure thoughts. And, as I mentioned before, impure thoughts can build a house in our minds that create a place for lust to transpire. Internal lust can lead to the desire for external release, causing us to look at things or even act on things that result in sin. Once they have been ignited, such desires can become a wild fire. Then, the need to satisfy the sexual urge may become unbearable.

The first thought or sight of something lustful or impure is not a sin. Nevertheless, just like the piece of wood used in the building of the house of thoughts, if we take a second look, it is like adding a second board to the house. This often leads to a third look, by which time; we are often lured into an act of immorality. This could involve looking blatantly at lustful or pornographic images, the act of finding ways to pleasure ourselves, or through getting a sexual release. (The same could be said from finding satisfaction from other impure sources, such as drugs, etc.) A popular song even states that the "second glance" is the one that causes the fall. When we are equipped with the "mind of Christ," we will be able to resist the second look. It is like taking one step into quick sand;

one leg may be sinking, but the other foot is still on solid ground. With that foot, you will be able to pull yourself back to safety. However, if you are two steps in, it will be much harder to retreat. Nothing is impossible; if you find yourself two steps in, "STOP!" retreat and return to your peace. Always watch were your feet step, so you can maintain solid ground and proper footing.

3. RUN!

How do we retreat? Run! Move! Get out of there! For instance, if you're watching TV and end-up viewing something impure, do not merely change the station; instead, get up and leave the room. If you're on the computer and you stumble across a bad website, don't just close it out—Leave! **Remove yourself from the tempting environment.** Likely, all you need to do is move, which allows you to refocus and find your freedom. If you're working and this happens, get up and go for a walk to clear your head. As you go, pray in the Spirit and declare that you are the righteousness of Christ. Incredibly, when you return, you will find that your mind has been unclouded.

One of the things that you should guard against is moving to a similar setting. One night, for example, I was watching TV when a sexual show started. I changed the channel, turned off the TV, and left the room. Victory! Right? Not-so-fast! I went into the office and turned on the computer. Next thing I knew, the temptation had followed me in there. The second temptation was much more of a battle. Finally, I mustered the strength to turn off the computer and leave the room. In order to change my environment, I went to soak in God's presence. Moral of the story: Don't run from one tempting environment straight into another. Consequently, if you're tempted on the TV, leaving the house and renting a movie won't help you much either. It's the same thing as taking the "second look" because your mind is not prepared to make a pure decision. Alternatively, go somewhere free of identical temptations.

Once you have removed yourself from the tempting environment, remove the residue of the environment from your mind. Flush the tempting thoughts and tear down any timbers that where built, by declaring truth and speaking freedom over your life. I, for instance, will say things either to myself, or about myself, such as: "Dave, protect your purity! Cleanse your mind and think like Jesus"; or "This isn't who I am—I am the righteousness of Christ; I am holy; I will think on things above and not on things below." I also speak the Word to myself. We would be wise to follow

David's lead and "strengthen ourselves in the Lord."

4. <u>Have Accountable Friendships</u>

Accountability must be based on a true relationship to be successful. Find someone who you trust and who can add strength to areas where you may be weak. If you are just reporting to a principal whom you are afraid of, then your premise will be to improve your actions, and not to change your heart, which controls your actions. Also, you cannot be accountable to someone who has major struggles in the same areas as you. You will both most likely fall, and then cry to each other about the experience. This may enable you to feel better momentarily, but it will eventually develop a pattern of fruitlessness.

You need someone who is strong in faith and who will be both tender and tough with you. He or she needs to be someone who is there to build you up, not to tear you down. It is wise to have accountability with someone of the same sex, especially concerning purity. I also recommend having more than one person to confide in. Find those who will "have-your-back." They will have a heart to cover sin and struggles, not a heart to expose. They must also have some level of authority in your life that has been developed through friendship. Often, they will be a pastor or mentor whose desire isn't to police you, but to protect you, keep you safe, and provide a comfortable place for you to confess and be restored. If you are dealing with something, they are the only ones who need to hear about it. There is no need to go around telling everyone that you screwed up. You're not a "screw up," you all are the sons and daughters of God. This remains true regardless of what you do. Surround yourself with trustworthy friends you can talk to and who remind you of who you are in Christ when you are experiencing a difficult season.

5. <u>RISE!</u>

If you do fall, fine. It's done. One mistake did not initiate the end of the world. You're not disqualified. It's not the end of your life, ministry, job, etc. God's heart is recovery. The only thing you need to focus on is finding your connection with Father, and running into His arms. He will take you and put His robe of forgiveness around you. Jesus shed His blood to make you clean and white as snow. (As Paul mentions in Romans 6; however, this doesn't give us a license to sin.) He loved you before you fell, and that love will cause you to rise.

Another thing to avoid if you have a mishap is the urge to go into hiding. Before I realized the level of freedom I currently live in, I dealt with a vicious cycle of temptation-sin-seclusion-depression. When I messed up, I would try to shield myself from the outside world. I didn't want to go to church or be around my friends because I felt unworthy. I was essentially avoiding the very assets designed to both restore me, and make me feel better. **The best thing you can do after rushing into Father's arms is to embrace fellowship with believers.**

Every time you and I stumble, it gives us reason to rise. Every time we rise it demonstrates that Jesus is risen from the dead and Lord over all. Dust off your feet and keep going. You have not gone backwards or failed a test. You lived life and now you will have more experience to live it better next time. This is all the more reason to rise. Therefore, rise you sons and daughters of God. Rise on the wings of eagles, as the Spirit takes you higher.

Conclusion

This list could have been vast; however, I simply wanted to give five practical and easy-to-remember steps that will help you to thrive. Purity is not what you do; it is what Jesus has done in you. If you base purity on what you do, then you are living from the Old Covenant. The most that amounts to is filthy rags. If your purity is what He has done, then you are living from the New Covenant, and are white as snow. This perspective is vital. Viewing it this way will cause you to look back and see victories where you used to see failures.

<u>Study Questions</u>

List the 5 Practical Steps to purity:

How do we "run?"

What is the best thing to do after rushing to Father?

<u>Notes</u>

4

The Purpose of Purity

What is the point of living purely? Should we do it because it is some sort of commandment? Is it what's expected of us as Christians? What is the purpose of purity? It is almost as though there is some standard that we all expect each other to live by, but deep down we feel it is something we will not fully accomplish. And, with much inclination, we suspect those around aren't able to either. I will be honest; this is not an easy question to answer. Much pondering and prayer would be required. It is almost like we know it's something that we should do, but we never really consider why. So here it goes—WHY?

Why Live Pure?

I am sure most of us would respond in a way that recites the expectations of Jesus and the Bible. Actually, this is a great starting point. Scripture does possess a call to purity. As one who loves the "fire of God" my thoughts lead me to verses that mention the refining of gold by fire. The purpose of this process is to make the gold more pure. In essence, the heat from the fire causes the impurities to rise to the surface. When this happens, the goldsmith can scrape them away, leaving a purer source of gold.

But who can endure the day of his coming, and who can stand when he appears? For he is like a refiner's fire and like fullers' soap. He will sit as a refiner and purifier of silver, and he will purify the sons of Levi and refine them like gold and silver, and they will bring offerings in righteousness to the Lord.

Malachi 3:2-3 ESV

The purpose of refining is to separate the elements. This illustration from Malachi describes the Lord's heart for the sons of Levi—the priest who ministered to God and to the people, to be purified like gold, so they would represent Him well. The impure elements in their lives needed to be scraped away; just as they are in the refining of the gold and silver. Such elements are of another nature. The more the impure nature is removed, the more the pure nature of the gold and the silver becomes evident.

Are you tracking? Every one knows that purer the gold is, the more valuable, shiny, and desirable it becomes; e.g. 12k and 24k. Gold, in and of itself, is the element. The goal of the refinement is to remove all entities except for one—gold. The outcome is to have it so refined that it is found in essence to be as it was created.

The Image of God

Who are we as beings on this planet? If you believe in Jesus, then you believe Father God created us in His image—the image of the Father, the Son, and the Holy Spirit. The following passage chronicles the creation:

Then God said, "Let us make man in our image, after our likeness.

So God created man in his own image, in the image of God he created him; male and female he created them.

Genesis 1:26a; 27 ESV

We are created in His image, which is the very reason why we are to live pure. God is our Source—the true element of our nature. Purity is relative to the element at hand; therefore, our purity is relative to the Element from which we were created, God Himself. The original state of mankind was crafted out of His own substance into His image. This is how we were in the beginning, and how we were intended to remain. Unfortunately, we messed that up and allowed ourselves to be influenced by something else. Any influence that doesn't originate in Him cannot be pure because it is borne of a foreign element. This was the introduction of an impurity into our nature. No longer were we pure gold. This fall created the need for all of us to be restored to the image of God; restored to the pure form of our creation.

For this reason, Jesus came as a Pure Source—Pure Gold. He lived with no impurities and remained true to His Source—His Father. In His perfection, He took our impurities upon Himself by giving us His purity. He then burned forever with the fires of heaven all the impurities that contaminated our nature with the sacrifice He made of His own pure life on the cross. Now and forever, we are pure, having been restored to the image of God through Jesus Christ.

So, where does that leave us trying to live purely if we already have been made pure? Exactly! We view ourselves as impure and therefore, because of the expectation of pseudo-religious demands, we strive to become something we already have been transformed into.

"Well then," why is it so hard to live pure? **I believe the struggle comes from living according to the image of fallen mankind rather than living according to the image of the risen Christ.** The old man is dead, as the book of Romans so repetitively reminds us, but the trick of enemy is to get us to believe that we are still in that condition. We will think as we believe and our bodies will respond according to how we think. When we think according to the image of God, we are drawing from that pure source and our lives will reflect His image. No longer will we resemble the image of the fallen nature because we both have been, and are being refined. This process continues as we begin to live correspondingly to this paradigm.

Wiping Away the Grime

We are pure. Purity is our nature. That is why it is difficult for us to sin. We sin and we feel bad because we chose to live in cohesion with an impure source. The difference between struggling with sin and sinning from our nature is the same difference between having to refine gold to remove the impurities, or simply buffing off the smudge that comes from everyday life. Jesus encapsulates this well at the last supper:

> Then he poured water into a basin and began to wash the disciples' feet and to wipe them with the towel that was wrapped around him. He came to Simon Peter, who said to him, "Lord, do you wash my feet?" Jesus answered him, "What I am doing you do not understand now, but afterward you will

understand." Peter said to him, "You shall never wash my feet." Jesus answered him, "If I do not wash you, you have no share with me." Simon Peter said to him, "Lord, not my feet only but also my hands and my head!" Jesus said to him, "The one who has bathed does not need to wash, except for his feet, but is completely clean. And you are clean..."

John 13:5-10 ESV

Peter was already clean. He just needed a touch from Jesus to wipe away the grime that comes with daily life. If you're driving down the road and bugs splatter on your windshield, you don't go and replace the whole thing do you? No, of course not! You simply turn on the wiper-wash and it cleans away the filth. The answer to the cleansing of the glass is built in. It is in the nature or design of the car for it to clean the windshield. It is the same with us. When we are born again, it is in our design for the Holy Spirit within us to wipe away the grime.

Why Shouldn't We do Whatever Feels Good?

Ah, herein lays the issue or the root of the matter regarding purity. I will give an attempt to answer it, but first, I want to share some responses I gained when I posted the question on Facebook, "Why should we try to live in purity?"

It's more fun! (David)

Ever drink water from a toilet? (David T.)

'Blessed are the pure in heart, for they shall see God.' I believe this verse is not (only) referring to the physical, but the spiritual eyes. When we walk in purity we have a clear visual of Christ and in that, are able to show Christ in and through us. (Brittany)

There's so much more peace there. You allow God to love you fully. And I agree... It's more fun. Really . . . it's not so much a "should" as it is a: YIPPEE! THIS IS AWESOME! WHY WOULD I WANT TO DO IT ANY OTHER WAY? That, and: I LOVE ME! I'M THIS AWESOME PIECE OF ART! WHY WOULD I WOULD I WANT TO DESTROY SOMETHING THIS ROCKIN' AMAZING!?! (Maggie)

Great responses! It seems the consensus is that living in purity just makes life better. Think about it, God created us in His image; as a result, things like sex and pleasure were created by Him too. That being the case, then there is a grand design for the fulfillment of such aspects of life. If we live out of who we are in Christ, then we can fulfill this experience in pure ways. Living the way He intended will breed satisfaction in our souls. Living the way of the fallen will only breed despair, guilt, and shame.

When we stray from living the way God created us to live, then it perverts His original design intended to give us maximum pleasure, fulfillment, release, and satisfaction in Him. The common misconception in the world is that a life of purity is no fun. On the contrary, when purity comes from living like Jesus, it's fantastic.

Conclusion

I feel like I am just getting started in the examination of our subject. I am having so much "fun" in the quest of understanding and walking in purity. In the next chapter, we will get into the benefits and power of living daily from the pure source of life. This will reinforce the necessity to live purely.

<u>Study Questions</u>

Why should we live purely?

Why do we struggle?

What happens when we stray from living the way God intended us to live?'

Notes

5

The Power of Purity

One of the benefits of living purely is power. Originally, I was going to state that purity produces power; however, as I proceed to study and consider the components of purity, I determined that purity is power. When purity is siphoned from the Pure Source, the Living Well, then it is in essence, the Power Source of the Universe. We have a Pure Source of Power—Holy Spirit—for every thing we do in this life. Fundamentally, living purely is living powerfully.

The Internal Change

I finished the last chapter, "The Purpose of Purity," by describing why we should live in purity while avoiding "whatever" feels good. When we try to put on purity like a jacket, it is the same as trying to cover our sins with acts of righteousness. This image looks good on the outside, but insecurity remains on the inside. **When purity comes from the inside, we don't have to put on anything on the outside because our inner nature has changed.**

Pureness in its perfection comes from the inside-out, not from the outside-in. If the latter were true, then the Law would've been sufficient means for our union with Christ. However, we know through Jesus that an internal divine intervention was essential. Relating to God from the outside-in is Old Covenant. Relating to God from the inside-out is New Covenant. Again, our spirits control the mind and the body. They were designed with the purpose of uniting with Holy Spirit. This union gives us the "mind of Christ," and enhances our cognizance of life. We will no longer think according to the flesh because the mind and the body are now in subjection to our spirits, causing our external actions to reflect His will, bringing us into harmony with God. A pure lifestyle becomes our nature and removes the struggle to "do it because we have to." The "end-product" is His purity becoming our purity, and we are liberated from trying to reach it through "works."

Pure Like God

In order to illuminate the importance of this inner transformation, I want to share a few more responses to the Facebook question I asked in the last chapter concerning why we should live purely:

> Pursuit of purity brings with it clarity of conscience. Just like pure clean water quenches thirst better than any other drink, a pure lifestyle breeds peace in the soul and mind. (John)

> A conscience at peace with God has more confidence in God and this is a key to all supernatural flow in the Spirit. (Mark)

> Because we are to be like God! (Alicia)

These answers give tremendous insight. As John describes, "a pure lifestyle breeds peace in the soul and mind." Mark really brings out a point that I have neglected up to now— PEACE. Purity brings peace. It's like pink bismuth for the soul because it soothes the mind and body from the intensities wrought in every-day life. Finally, Alicia really nails the perspective I am presenting, "Because we are to be like God." **I think this is the most vital piece in understanding why we are to live pure, being like God!** Living from His world immerses earth with the pure life of heaven.

The Spirit of Power that ignited the universe when God declared, "Let there be light," is the same Spirit that dwells within us. The more we draw from this Well, the more pure and powerful we become. We need to recognize the purity inside us. This will transform our minds and transfigure our bodies into the image of Christ. Pure water will flow from us and bring healing life to every person or situation we encounter. It's more than simply resisting a thought or temptation; it's a reformation of the thought patterns of society and culture.

Private Victories enable us to become Public Conquerors

David killed the lion and the bear when no one was looking, which perpetually prepared him to stand against the giant when the future of his nation depended on it. The rest of the army was afraid because they looked at Goliath with their eyes and not with their hearts. Their bodies were controlling their spirits, revealing that in this instance, they were drinking impure water. David, on the other hand, had not only been drinking, but also bathing in the pure springs of heaven. He was not dehydrated when the day of triumph came because his spirit had been fully irrigated with heavenly water.

This is how we were created, to live in victory. Break the rhythm of failure after failure. From now on, I declare that you will leap from victory to victory. You will be like David, going forth from the lion, to the bear, to the giant, to the kingdom. You will overcome!

Conclusion

The focus of this chapter was the power that comes from living purely within. The next chapter will reveal the secret dangers of compromising our true nature, which will enable us to recognize the origins of impurity, and empower us to overcome it.

<u>Study Questions</u>

How does our inner nature change?

What is the most vital piece in why we
are to live pure?

Notes

6

Dangers of Impurity

Another way to protect your purity is to understand the temptation's source of origin. Our flesh is a powerful force that is to be managed towards our current or future spouses. The lust of the flesh, without management, will burn like fire until it finds fulfillment. The bible warns against being carried away by this desire. It can come from within if the mind isn't renewed, it can come from the world, or it can come from the devil.

But I say, walk by the Spirit, and you will not gratify the desires of the flesh.

Galatians 5:16 ESV

The enemy targets these desires in an attempt to make us stumble. It's essential that we learn to direct ourselves, or we will sin out of internal desire to satisfy our flesh. However, not every temptation spawns from this desire. In my experience, temptation often comes as an attack against my relationship with God. In the book of Ephesians, the Apostle Paul urges us to put on the armor of God so that we will be able stand firm against the plans and attacks from the evil spiritual world.

Finally, be strong in the Lord and in the strength of his might. Put on the whole armor of God, that you may be able to stand against the schemes of the devil. For we do not wrestle against flesh and blood, but against the rulers, against the authorities, against the cosmic powers over this present darkness, against the spiritual forces of evil in the heavenly places.

Ephesians 6:10-12 ESV

Temptations are Demonic

This passage reveals that temptations originate from evil forces. Realizing this will cause us to recognize the temptation as it an assault against our purity. Sexual immorality and pornography are schemes of the devil. And, this may sound shocking, but sexual immorality and pornography are demonic principalities designed to cause creation to warp its perception of both God and themselves. In doing so, creation will feel unworthy of pleasing "task-master" God. The first assignment against the believer is to hinder their walk with God by making them feel that real satisfaction comes from one of the impure sources. The end-goal is to get the believer to backslide and turn away from God. Simplistically, evil wants to invade your mind with impure thoughts. These thoughts are the elements sent to tarnish the pure gold of our hearts.

If a sexual image tempts you, view it as an attack trying to stifle your relationship with Jesus. This perspective will make the temptation less appetizing. As I mentioned in the second chapter, simply seeing something isn't sin. The image is a "flaming dart" that seeks to build a house of thoughts in your mind. The recognition of the attack prevents the dart from lodging in your thought process.

False Pleasure

All sexual immorality is false pleasure. It can be wrapped in any package: soft-porn, hardcore, lust, homosexuality, graphic fantasies, adult magazines, seductive artwork, fornication, adultery, etc. They are designed to rob you of true pleasure and fulfillment. No matter how many times you find pleasures in these things, they will never truly satisfy, causing you to plunge deeper into an immoral lifestyle. This will cause you to search and search for fulfillment without ever realizing it. Breaking the cycle comes through living from the Pure Source. This satisfies the soul and gives you the strength to resist.

Sexual Sin is Sinning Against the Body

This passage clearly details why sexual sin is so dangerous and contrary to the heart of God:

> "All things are lawful for me," but not all things are helpful. "All things are lawful for me," but I will not be enslaved by anything... The body is not meant for sexual immorality, but for the Lord, and the Lord for the body. Do you not know that your bodies are members of Christ? Shall I then take the members of Christ and make them members of a prostitute? Never! Or do you not know that he who is joined to a prostitute becomes one body with her? For, as it is written, "The two will become one

flesh." But he who is joined to the Lord becomes one spirit with him.

1 Corinthians 6:12-13; 15-17 ESV

We were created to be one with God. Wow! That in itself is fuel enough to be strong. If we are one with Him, then we should not make immoral connections with our bodies.

The Triune Connection

The first reason sexual sin is a sin against the body is because it creates an impure triune connection.

"For this reason a man will leave his father and mother and be united to his wife, and the two will become one flesh." This is a profound mystery—but I am talking about Christ and the church.

Ephesians 5:31-32 ESV

Remember, Father, Son, and Spirit made us in His image. He connects to us through body, mind, and spirit. We are designed to have one connection of body, mind, and spirit with our spouses. We relate to them the way God relates to us.

> Flee from sexual immorality. Every other sin a person commits is outside the body, but the sexually immoral person sins against his own body. Or do you not know that your body is a temple of the Holy Spirit within you, whom you have from God? You are not your own, for you were bought with a price. So glorify God in your body.

> vv 18-20

Sex is so wonderful and pure in covenant marriage because it is connected to our bodies, our minds, and our spirits. Our body connects to our spouse, our mind connects to our spouse, and our spirit connects to our spouse. Unfortunately, an impure attachment also connects itself to our entire beings. Sexual release gives a pleasurable response that affects all of "us." Sex is connected to love, which also gives fulfillment and release to the body, the mind, and the spirit. An impure fulfillment of this throws our entire being off kilter. This is why sexual sin is sin against the body. Other ways to sin, while they are to be avoided, do not affect the body in the same way.

Holy Spirit makes His home in us. We are His temple, His dwelling. We are the most satisfied and fulfilled when His presence guides our lives. Glorifying God by living the way He intends brings true pleasure.

The power of Imagery

The second reason sexual sin is sin against the body is because of the effects of imagery. Pornography is an exposure of something intended to be between a man and a women in private. When we watch others in sexual acts, it results in a response in our bodies similar to what I previously described. The images become associated in our minds with release and fulfillment. If we view others conducting indecent acts beyond the natural order, then those images also attach. This causes us to think differently. It's like the opposite of renewing the mind because we begin to fire from this reality in relation to sexual fulfillment.

Secular and Christian studies have shown that pornographic imagery forms new pathways on the surface of the brain creating thought patterns that coincide with the images. If left unchecked, this perspective can form spectacles that warp our view of God, our spouses, and ourselves. We may, inevitably, find ourselves placing unrealistic expectations on our spouses that subconsciously imitate things we've seen in pornography. And, if you're single, it will warp your perception of true pleasure in marriage while creating false expectations of the opposite sex.

Virtual Reality

Pornography is virtual reality. Covenant marriage is true reality. Exposing the origin of the temptation reveals this to be true. Pornography tries to get you to live in a world that doesn't exist. If the problem is not solved, it leads to trying to create a world that fulfills these fantasies. Next, it can lead to living a lifestyle that mirrors what was watched. You will find yourself moving from spectator to participant. This is the goal of the persuasion. The devil isn't just satisfied with you watching; he wants you to join the club by turning fantasy into reality. Viewing a little porn on the Internet is intended to get you involved in fornications, orgies, and all other kinds of sexual sin. It is a manifestation of hell on earth, an illusion that offers false happiness.

The sight to see sin for what it really is liberates your interest in it. No one sees a sewage canal and thinks to himself or herself, "Oh boy, I want to take a big drink of that," or "Look at this great swimming pool." It's filth! It's gross! It's disgusting and would make us sick. The same goes for sexual immorality. View it like that, and your desire to drink from an impure source will evaporate.

Conclusion

I write without condemnation in mind as my goal is to literate freedom. It doesn't matter how far you've gone, victory is always waiting at the Mercy Seat—the loving feet of Jesus. I am also writing with experience, I too have dealt with bouts of pornography and sexual immorality. My personal freedom is based on the principles I am sharing with you. Like we read in Corinthians, Jesus purchased us with a price, His blood, which is more powerful than all the sins you've ever committed. There is always forgiveness. The most important step is to rise again if you fall.

This chapter has uncovered the origins of sexual sin, and how it affects living a pure lifestyle. In the final chapter I will focus on living out the pure lifestyle in radical ways, as one who is on fire for Jesus! We are not just on defensive; we are on the attack every time we resist temptation.

> Submit yourselves therefore to God. Resist the devil, and he will flee from you.

James 4:7 ESV

Submitted to God is living from the Pure Source. Our resistance is our attack, which renders the devil powerless to gain ground in our minds. As a result, he has no choice but to flee!

Recommendation for Further Help and Ministry

If sexual sin has been an issue for you, I strongly urge you get Bethel based Sozo ministry. The focus of this ministry is to connect you to the Godhead: Father, Son, and Holy Spirit. Visit www.bethelsozo.com for more info.

Study Questions

Where does temptation originate when it's not of the flesh?

What are the two ways sexual sin is sinning against the body?

What happens when we see sin for what it really is?

Notes

7

Protecting Purity

The content from the first six chapters collectively form a shield. This shield is designed to help you protect yourself against compromising temptations. The goal is to invoke an offensive response; one that wields a sword in the midst of the battle through knowledge of the enemy's tactics.

The Offensive

The exposition of his plans and schemes were examined in the last chapter. Now, we will go on the offensive. Let's take a closer look at the armor of God and learn how to creatively activate our weaponry:

> Therefore take up the whole armor of God, that you may be able to withstand in the evil day, and having done all, to stand firm. Stand therefore, having fastened on the belt of truth, and having put on the breastplate of righteousness, and, as shoes for your feet, having put on the readiness given by the gospel of peace. In all circumstances, take up the shield of faith, with which you can extinguish all the flaming darts of the evil one; and take the helmet of

salvation, and the sword of the Spirit, which is the word of God.

Ephesians 6:13-17 ESV

The armor of God contains defensive pieces that protect the body. It also contains an offensive piece: **We are armed with the sword of the Spirit.** When in the midst of battle, only using a shield equates to dancing around and dodging the onslaught. You need a weapon in your hands. The weapon is the Sword of the Spirit, which cuts down the enemy's forces! Knowing his schemes exposes his weakness, showing us precisely where to strike. The awareness that we are not fighting flesh and blood, but demonic armies— disguised as tempting imagery and false pleasures—gives us knowledge of his movement. This enables us to both counteract and counterattack. Not only that, but we can also attack his plans before they are used to attack us. It's like killing the archer before he releases the arrow from the bow.

I gave five practical steps to walk out purity in chapter three. This list can defensively help in escaping a situation and offensively assist in its avoidance.

> For at the window of my house I have looked out through my lattice, and I have seen among the simple, I have perceived among the youths, a young man lacking sense, passing along the street near her corner, taking the road to her house in the twilight, in the evening, at the time of night and darkness.

> Proverbs 7:6-9 ESV

This verse is so telling of a circumstance that could have been avoided. Wisdom reveals that we should steer clear places where we know temptation waits for us. This is an offensive approach; taking the temptation out before we walk down the road and find ourselves in a desperate attempt to defend our purity.

If you often get tempted on the computer, sandwich the time you spend on it in prayer. If it's the TV, then do likewise. If magazines tempt you, then don't go down that isle when you're at the grocery store or the bookshop. If you need to get something there, before you go, prophesy strength over the time spent. Paul ends his elaboration of the armor of God with the enforcement, "Pray at all times in the spirit." This act will activate a heavenly perspective that causes you and me to see clearly in the normality of life.

Protecting Your Engagement

If you are dating or engaged, it is a special time to preserve your purity and ensure that the wedding night is a fantastic and amazing experience. If you have already compromised, reset the relationship with pure standards. Set up a purity plan with friends and leaders you trust to hold you accountable and keep a safe watch over your soul. If you have a hard time controlling passion around each other, take a radical approach in this area as well. Don't find yourselves alone in environments that ignite passion. Look for ways to avoid this scenario. Declare purity over your relationship. Read great books on the subject, be accountable, and get pre-marital counseling. <u>Decide that a pure lifestyle will be the future history of your engagement.</u> Be creative in ways that uniquely apply to your lives.

Practical Steps for a Purity Plan

1. Avoid Tempting Environments

2. Make Prophetic Declarations

3. Be Accountable

4. Pre-Marital Counseling

5. Be Creative

All of the examples I mentioned, both in regard to personal purity and maintaining a pure relationship, are pro-active. This is a zealous tactic that says "I will not find myself in a tempting situation where I need to quickly escape." **Don't wait to unsheathe the Sword of the Spirit until enemies surround you—Ready it in advance!**

Clean House

Let's be radical! Let's be extreme in our pursuit and preservation of purity. **One way to be radical is to "clean house," both mentally and literally.** Let's rid ourselves of all defilement and cleanse ourselves of impure influences. Dump the movies, and delete the files. Gently sever any impure relationships. If you're married, commit purity to one another. If you need counseling or a Sozo, set it up quickly. Today is the day for freedom. Yesterday is gone, and the history of impurity is washed away in the love and faithfulness of Jesus. Wear your purity like a badge of freedom. Let this verse remove any "hint" of sexual immorality from your lifestyle.

But sexual immorality and all impurity or covetousness must not even be named among you, as is proper among saints.

I'm not being legalistic. I am not recommending that we walk around like robots:

"Must ... Avoid ... Temptation, Compute ... Compute"

(in robot voice)

Don't go around acting weird. You are free. However, if you feel something impure tug on your heart, check it and flush it. The smallest image or thought unchecked will become a seed, waiting to sprout at just the moment of weakness. Replace the lie with the truth, and the impure source with the Pure Source.

Purity is walked out differently by each individual. Paul explains this in the same chapter I mentioned earlier from Corinthians. Something may tug on your heart that has no affect on another. Yes, there is a line of truth we all must live by, but different things will affect different people in different ways. We all must listen to our conscience—our transformed minds. Holy Spirit is our Comforter, He convicts us to rise when we fall. He is also our Guide, who leads us beside pure waters. He sees all attacks before they come and will always graciously point us in the right direction. Listen to His voice.

Your past is erased. You are a champion. You are an overcomer. "Your identity is not found in who you were, it's found in who you are becoming," Graham Cooke. The real you is a son and a daughter of the King.

Closing Prayer

Lord, enable and empower us to draw every day from You—The Pure Source—The Living Water of Eternal Life. Make me, and the brothers and sisters who read these words strong in spirit, mind, and action. No more perversions God. Strengthen us to steward the time we have in the dark—when no one is looking—so we will not stumble when we are scheduled to step into the light.

Lord, bring healing and comfort to all who have struggled with purity. Enable us to "go and sin no more" because we are drinking from the Pure Source. Saturate us in Your pureness. From now on, protecting a pure lifestyle will be something that we are able to live out with ease. No more burdens on those who struggle. Place in them the resilience to rise!

Transform our minds to become like the mind of Jesus. Increase the power in your people, and open our eyes to see who we really are in You, in the Spirit, and in the earth. In Jesus Name!

The New You Now Begins ...

<u>Review for Dating or Engaged Couples</u>*

List the 5 practical steps for a purity plan:

What can be decided about the engagement?

*These answers are underlined within the chapter.

Notes for Relationships

<u>Study Questions</u>

What is the offensive weapon listed in the armor of God?

When should we unsheathe our swords?

What is one way to be radical?

<u>Notes</u>

About the Author

David Edwards is a speaks at churches and conferences, igniting passion for supernatural Christianity. He teaches at Bethel Atlanta School of Supernatural Ministry. He lives Newnan, GA with his dashing wife Allessia. If you would like to invite David to speak at a church or conference:

Revivalism.net/invite

Dave@Revivalism.net

Revivalism.net

Books by David W Edwards

Activating a Prophetic Lifestyle

The Call for Revivalists

**Available on Amazon.com and
Booksellers Worldwide**

63421539R00065

Made in the USA
Charleston, SC
04 November 2016